WEATHER
Infographics

Chris Oxlade

Chicago, Illinois

© 2014 Raintree
an imprint of Capstone Global Library, LLC
Chicago, Illinois

To contact Capstone Global Library, please
call 800-747-4992, or visit our web site
www.capstonepub.com

Edited by Rebecca Rissman, Dan Nunn, and John-Paul Wilkins
Designed by Philippa Jenkins
Original illustrations © Capstone Global Library Ltd 2014
Illustrations by HL Studios
Picture research by Elizabeth Alexander
Production by Vicki Fitzgerald
Originated by Capstone Global Library Ltd

Library of Congress Cataloging-in-Publication Data
Oxlade, Chris.
  Weather / Chris Oxlade.
    pages cm.—(Infographics)
  Includes bibliographical references and index.
  ISBN 978-1-4109-6219-5 (hardback)—ISBN 978-1-4109-6224-
9 (paperback) 1. Graphic methods—Juvenile literature. 2. Charts,
diagrams, etc.—Juvenile literature. 3. Weather—Juvenile literature. 4.
Meteorology—Juvenile literature. I. Title.
  QA90.O959 2014
  551.6072'8—dc23   2013012536

Acknowledgments
We would like to thank the following for permission to reproduce
photographs: Capstone Global Library p. 4; Shutterstock pp. 4 (©
M.Stasy, © Pakhnyushcha, © Stella Caraman, © Thomas Bethge),
8 (© Alhovik), 9 (© Smit).

We would like to thank Diana Bentley and Marla Conn for their
invaluable help in the preparation of this book.

Every effort has been made to contact copyright holders
of any material reproduced in this book. Any omissions
will be rectified in subsequent printings if notice is given to
the publisher.

Disclaimer
All the Internet addresses (URLs) given in this book were valid at the
time of going to press. However, due to the dynamic nature of the
Internet, some addresses may have changed, or sites may have
changed or ceased to exist since publication. While the author
and publisher regret any inconvenience this may cause readers, no
responsibility for any such changes can be accepted by either the
author or the publisher.

Metric Conversions

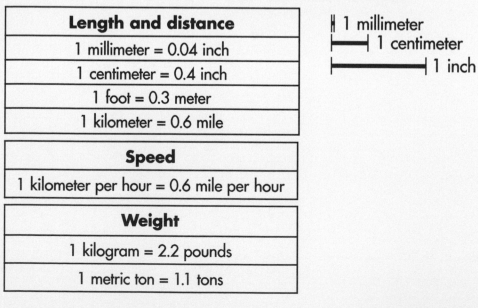

Length and distance
1 millimeter = 0.04 inch
1 centimeter = 0.4 inch
1 foot = 0.3 meter
1 kilometer = 0.6 mile

Speed
1 kilometer per hour = 0.6 mile per hour

Weight
1 kilogram = 2.2 pounds
1 metric ton = 1.1 tons

CONTENTS

Some words are shown in bold, **like this**. You can find out what they mean by looking in the glossary.

ABOUT INFOGRAPHICS

An infographic is a picture that gives you information. Infographics can be graphs, charts, maps, or other sorts of pictures. The infographics in this book are about weather.

Infographics make information easier to understand. We see infographics all over the place, every day. They appear in books, in newspapers, on television, on web sites, on posters, and in advertisements.

Weather for the week

Here is an example of a weather infographic. It shows what the weather might be like for the next week in a particular place.

WHAT IS WEATHER?

Weather can be sunny or cloudy, wet or dry, warm or cold, or windy or **calm**. It can also be a mixture of lots of these things! We use different symbols to show different types of weather.

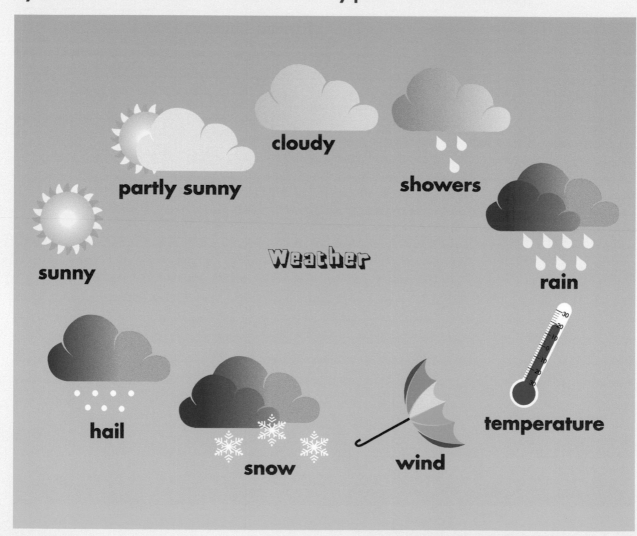

cloudy

partly sunny

showers

sunny

Weather

rain

hail

snow

wind

temperature

World record weather

Some places in the world are very hot or very cold. Some are very wet and some are very dry. Some are very windy. This map shows some world-record weather around the world.

Sunniest place on Earth
Yuma, Arizona
11.4 hours of sunshine per day on **average**

Hottest place on Earth
Death Valley, California
134.1°F (highest)

Wettest place on Earth
Mawsynram, India
467 inches of rain per year

Driest place on Earth
Arica, Chile
0.03 inches of rain per year

Coldest place on Earth
Vostock, Antarctica
−128.6°F (lowest)

Windiest place on Earth
George V Coast, Antarctica
200 miles per hour

TEMPERATURE

How warm today?

Weather experts record the **temperature** regularly throughout the day and night. This is an example of a 24-hour temperature record. It shows how hot or cold it was every three hours, from midday on February 1 to midday on February 2, 2012, in Pittsburgh, Pennsylvania.

Temperature in degrees Fahrenheit

12 p.m.	3 p.m.	6 p.m.	9 p.m.	12 a.m.	3 a.m.	6 a.m.	9 a.m.	12 p.m.
52°F	**55.9°F**	**53.1°F**	**45°F**	**39°F**	**36°F**	**36°F**	**36°F**	**39.9°F**

How warm this week?

Weather experts record the weather all over the world every day. This graph shows the average temperature in London, England, on each day for a week in September 2012.

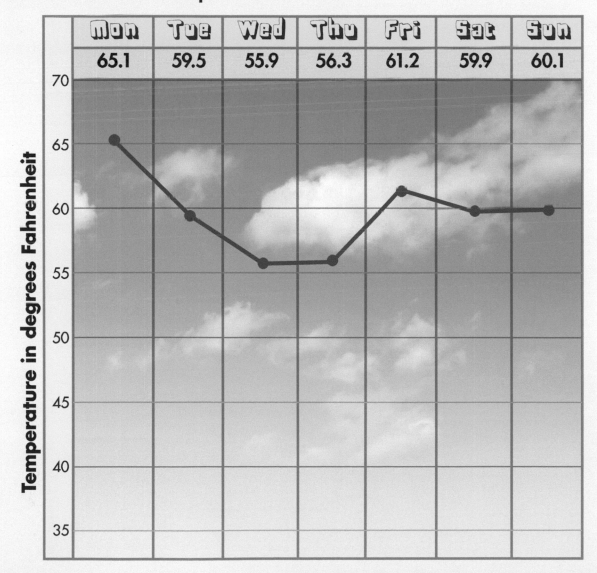

Mon	Tue	Wed	Thu	Fri	Sat	Sun
65.1	59.5	55.9	56.3	61.2	59.9	60.1

TYPES OF WEATHER

How much rain this week?

This is an example of a weekly rainfall chart. It shows how much rain fell each day for a week.

4.3mm	2.9mm	9.5mm	2.4mm	0.3mm	0.2mm	0mm
Mon	Tue	Wed	Thu	Fri	Sat	Sun

Rainfall in millimeters

The heaviest rain

Sometimes it rains very heavily. This chart shows some of the heaviest downpours ever.

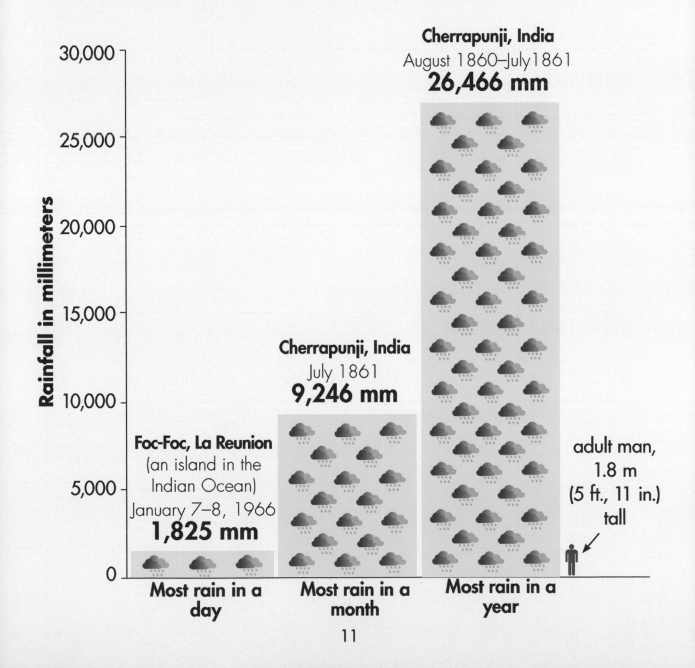

Rainfall in millimeters

Cherrapunji, India
August 1860–July1861
26,466 mm

Cherrapunji, India
July 1861
9,246 mm

Foc-Foc, La Reunion
(an island in the Indian Ocean)
January 7–8, 1966
1,825 mm

adult man,
1.8 m
(5 ft., 11 in.)
tall

Most rain in a day

Most rain in a month

Most rain in a year

The biggest hail

Hail is made up of lumps of ice that fall from clouds. The lumps are called hailstones. Some hailstones are enormous. This map shows where some of the worst hailstorms have taken place.

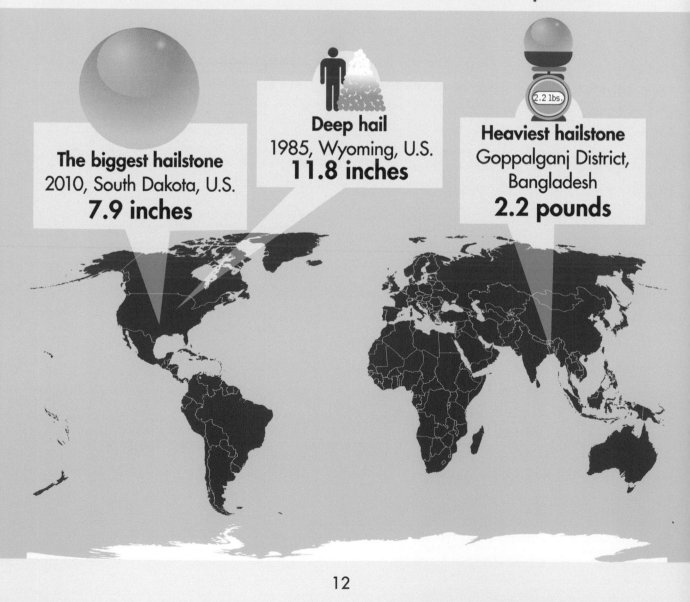

The biggest hailstone
2010, South Dakota, U.S.
7.9 inches

Deep hail
1985, Wyoming, U.S.
11.8 inches

Heaviest hailstone
Goppalganj District,
Bangladesh
2.2 pounds

2.2 lbs.

How snowy?

The amount of snow that falls is measured by how deep the snow gets on the ground. This chart shows the amount of snow that fell each month in Banff, Canada, in 2006.

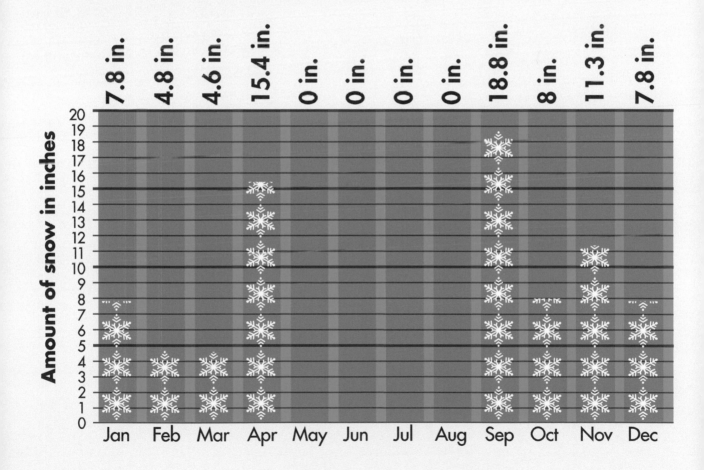

How windy?

Weather experts measure two things about the wind. They measure the strength of the wind and which way the wind is blowing. This chart shows how the strength and direction of the wind at Sydney Airport, Australia, changed during a day.

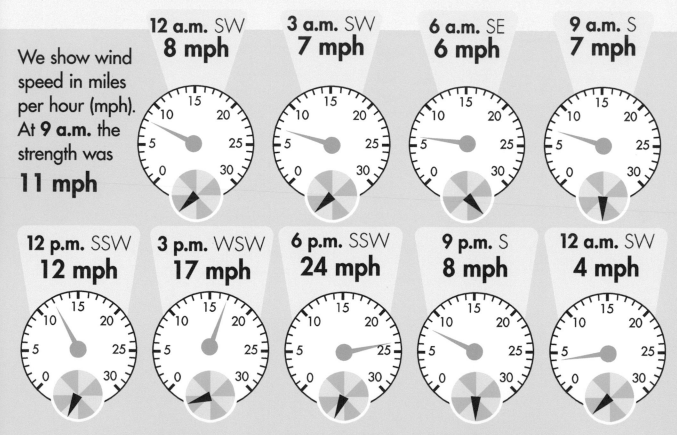

We show wind speed in miles per hour (mph). At **9 a.m.** the strength was **11 mph**

12 a.m. SW	3 a.m. SW	6 a.m. SE	9 a.m. S
8 mph	**7 mph**	**6 mph**	**7 mph**

12 p.m. SSW	3 p.m. WSW	6 p.m. SSW	9 p.m. S	12 a.m. SW
12 mph	**17 mph**	**24 mph**	**8 mph**	**4 mph**

We show wind direction with the points of a **compass**.
At **9 a.m.** the wind was blowing from north to south.

14

How sunny?

This is an example of a sunshine chart. It shows how many hours of sunshine there were each day for a week.

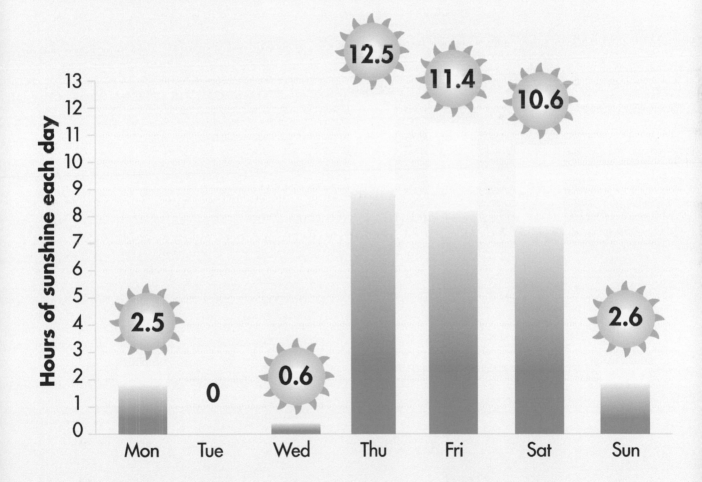

CLOUDS

Cloud shapes and sizes

Clouds come in many different shapes and sizes. This chart shows some of the clouds you might see when you look at the sky.

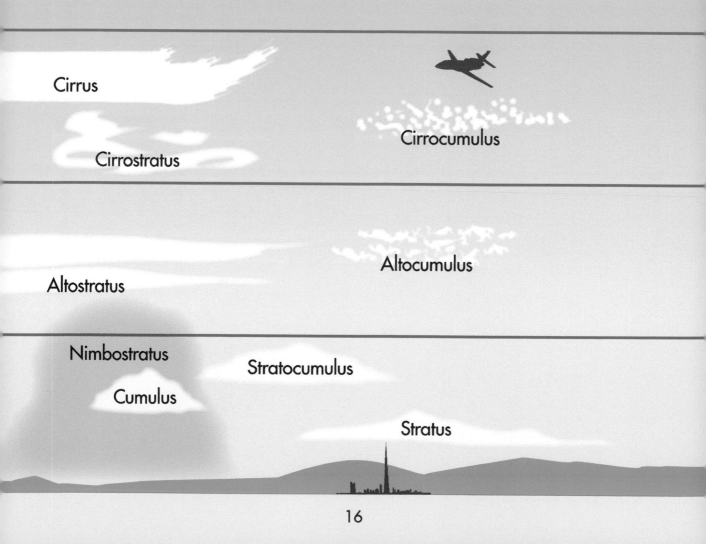

Cirrus

Cirrostratus

Cirrocumulus

Altostratus

Altocumulus

Nimbostratus

Stratocumulus

Cumulus

Stratus

Clouds are named by their shape and how high in the sky they are.

High-level clouds

10,000 meters
(32,808 feet)

Medium-level clouds

6,000 meters
(19,685 feet)

Altitude

Low-level clouds

2,000 meters
(6,560 feet)

Cumulonimbus

Thunder and lightning facts

Thunderstorms are giant clouds full of electricity. This infographic is about **thunder** and **lightning**.

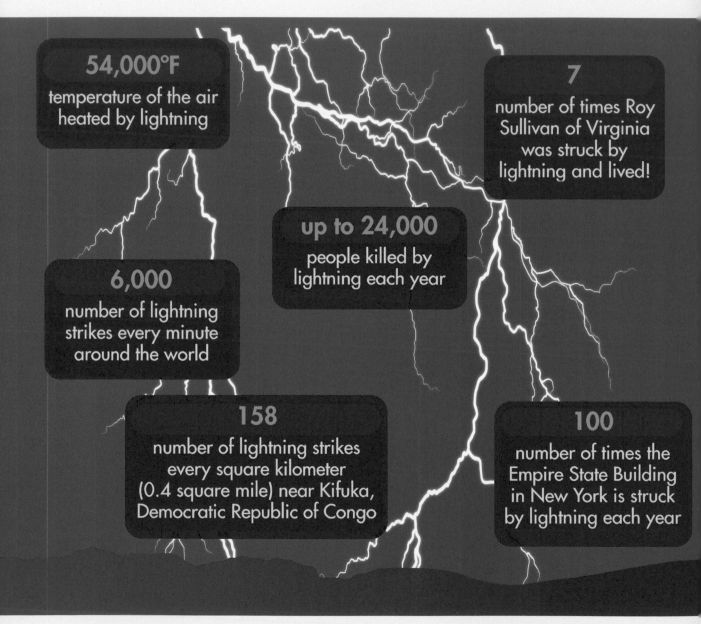

54,000°F
temperature of the air heated by lightning

7
number of times Roy Sullivan of Virginia was struck by lightning and lived!

up to 24,000
people killed by lightning each year

6,000
number of lightning strikes every minute around the world

158
number of lightning strikes every square kilometer (0.4 square mile) near Kifuka, Democratic Republic of Congo

100
number of times the Empire State Building in New York is struck by lightning each year

Thunder map

This map shows which areas of the world get the most thunderstorms.

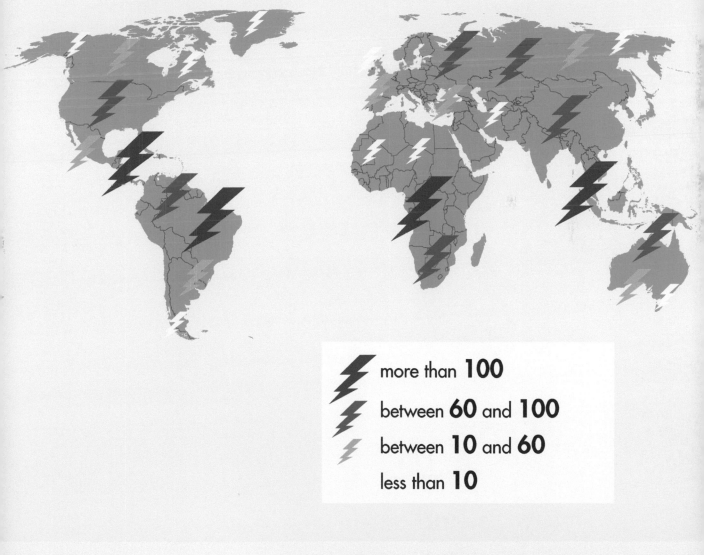

Number of days with thunder in a year

more than **100**

between **60** and **100**

between **10** and **60**

less than **10**

EXTREME WEATHER

Hurricanes

A hurricane is a giant swirling storm. Hurricanes start over the sea and sometimes hit land. They can cause terrible destruction. This infographic is about hurricanes.

A hurricane from above

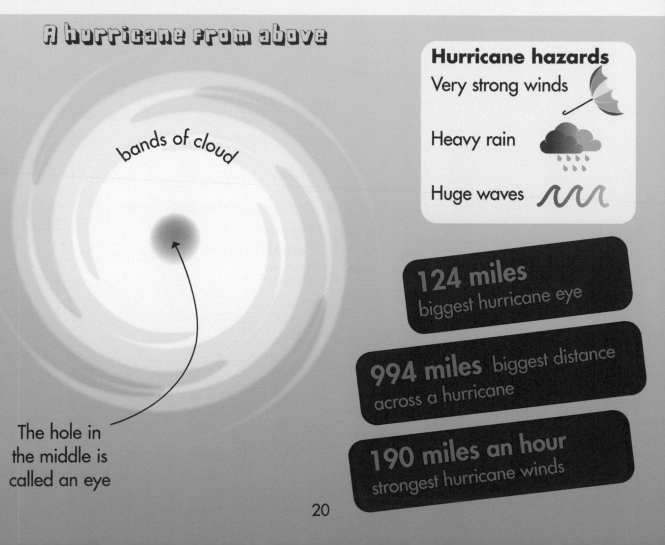

bands of cloud

The hole in the middle is called an eye

Hurricane hazards

Very strong winds

Heavy rain

Huge waves

124 miles
biggest hurricane eye

994 miles biggest distance across a hurricane

190 miles an hour
strongest hurricane winds

Where hurricanes strike

Hurricanes are called cyclones and typhoons in some parts of the world. They form near the equator. This map shows where hurricanes start and the paths they follow.

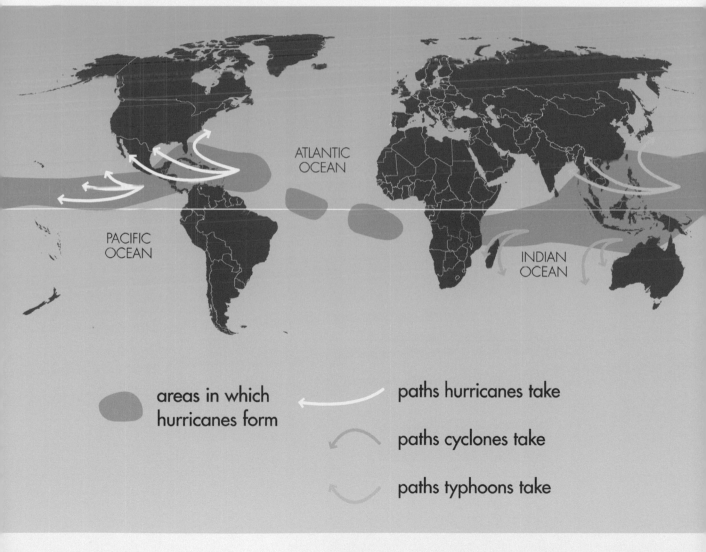

ATLANTIC
OCEAN

PACIFIC
OCEAN

INDIAN
OCEAN

areas in which hurricanes form

paths hurricanes take

paths cyclones take

paths typhoons take

Tornado facts

This infographic is about tornadoes. A tornado is a funnel-shaped storm. It spins very fast, making super strong winds. Tornadoes always hang down from giant thunderstorms.

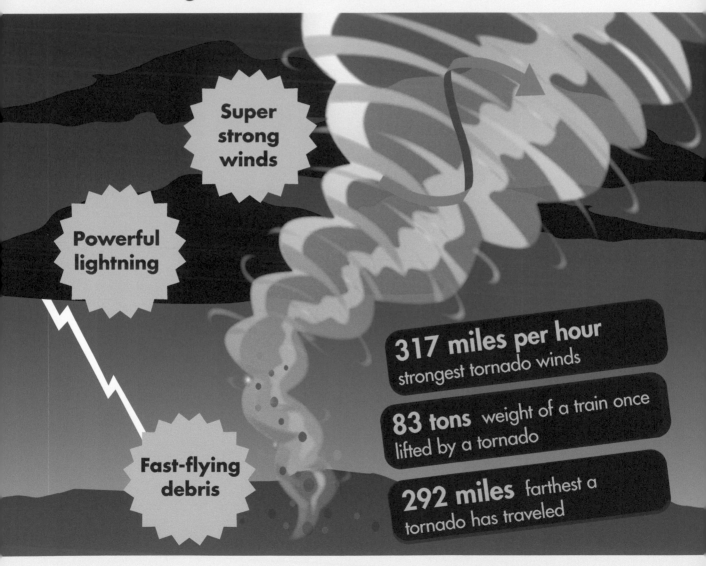

Super strong winds

Powerful lightning

Fast-flying debris

317 miles per hour strongest tornado winds

83 tons weight of a train once lifted by a tornado

292 miles farthest a tornado has traveled

Tornado Alley

Tornadoes happen in many places around the world, but the most famous place is an area of the United States known as Tornado Alley. This map shows where Tornado Alley is.

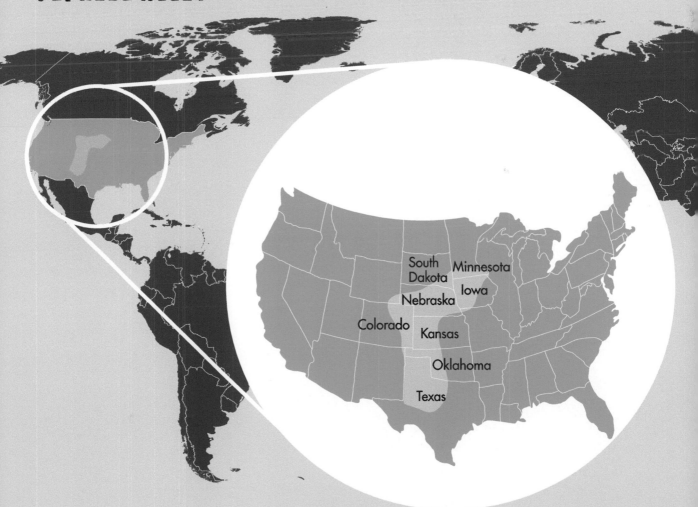

Tornado Alley

South Dakota
Minnesota
Iowa
Nebraska
Colorado
Kansas
Oklahoma
Texas

CLIMATES

Climate is the pattern of weather over time. We show climates by how much rain falls during a year, and what the temperature is over a year. This chart shows how much rain normally falls each month of the year in a certain place.

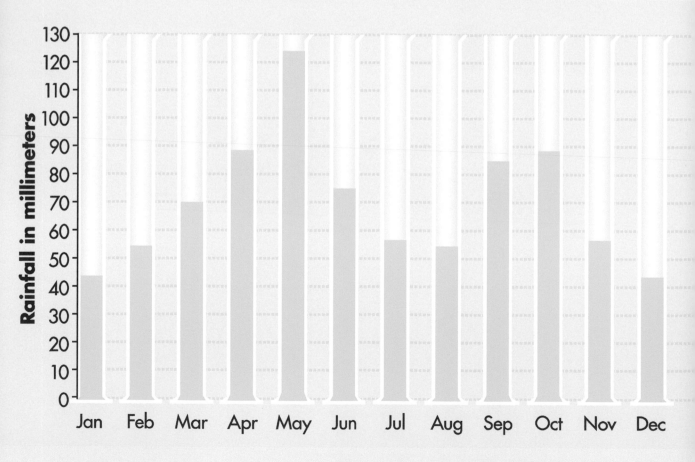

Temperature each month

This line graph shows the average temperature in Manchester, England, for each month for a year. It shows how the temperature rises and falls.

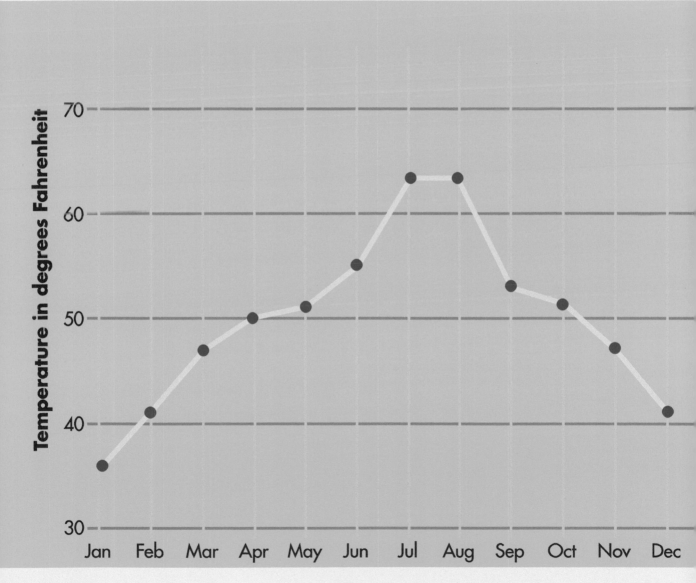

Climates around the world

This map shows what the climate is like in different parts of the world.

Polar very cold all year round

Temperate warm summers and cool winters

Desert very dry all year round

Tropical warm and rainy all year round

Mediterranean hot summers and warm winters

Mountains cold and snowy all year round

WEATHER FORECASTING

Weather forecasting means figuring out what the weather might be like for the next few days. This information is shown with weather maps. This is an example of a weather forecast map. You can see what weather will be like where you live.

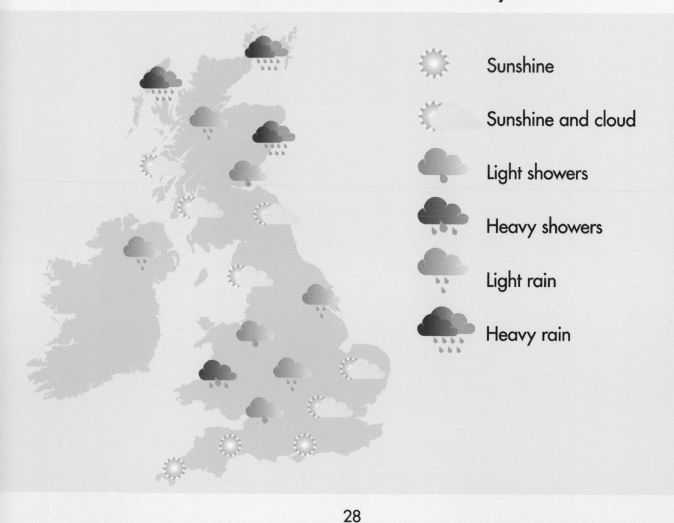

Sunshine

Sunshine and cloud

Light showers

Heavy showers

Light rain

Heavy rain

Weather for the week

This chart is an example of a five-day forecast. It shows in words and pictures what the weather will probably be like in the daytime for the next five days in a particular place.

Five-day forecast

Day	Weather	Max. Day (°F)	Min. Night (°F)	Wind (mph)
Mon		82	55	6
Tue		86	59	5
Wed		77	54	8
Thu		73	52	10
Fri		81	57	7

GLOSSARY

average sum of adding a set of numbers together and then dividing by the number of numbers in the set

calm not windy

climate pattern of weather that a place has over a long time

compass instrument for showing direction. A compass has a magnetic needle that points north.

lightning natural electricity produced in thunderclouds. Lightning appears as a bright flash or streak of light in the sky.

temperature how hot or cold something is

thunder booming noise that follows a flash of lightning

FIND OUT MORE

Books

Bodach, Vijaya. Making Graphs (series). Mankato, Minn.: Capstone, 2008.

Furgang, Kathy. *Everything Weather* (Everything). Washington, D.C.: National Geographic, 2012.

Ganeri, Anita. *Wild Weather* (Extreme Nature). Chicago: Raintree, 2013.

INDEX